downtown bookworks

INSECT-O-MANIA

BY ALLYSON
KULAVIS

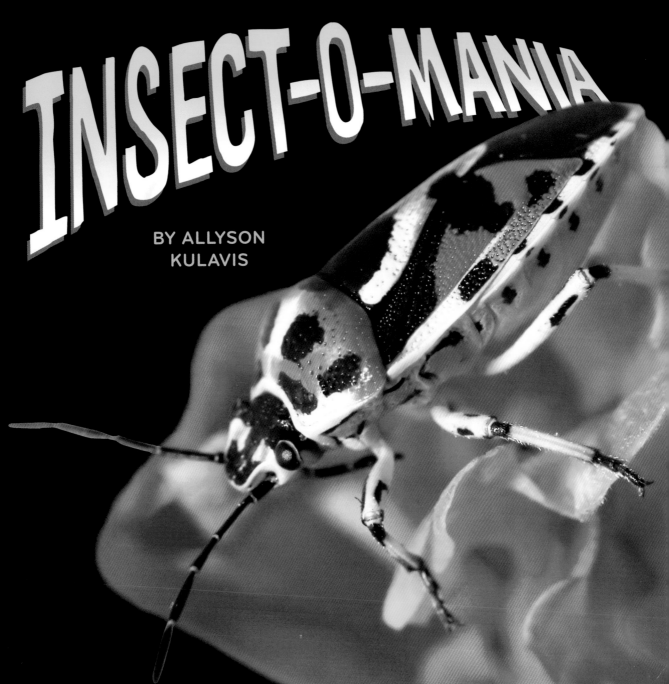

downtown bookworks

Entomologist consultant: Frederique Lavoipierre

Designed by Georgia Rucker
Typeset in Bryant Pro and Warugaki

PHOTO CREDITS Cover: liou.zojan/Shutterstock.com.
Interior: 1: Andre Goncalves/Shutterstock.com. Interior: 3: ©Minden Pictures/SuperStock. 4: defpicture/Shutterstock.com (lantern fly), Matt Jeppson/Shutterstock.com (grasshopper). 5: Minden Pictures/SuperStock (entomologist), Gucio_55/Shutterstock.com (stink bug), Roman Prokorov/Shutterstock.com (cockchafer), Linda Johnsonbaugh/Shutterstock.com (caterpillar). 6: Cosmin Manci/Shutterstock.com (cuckoo wasp), sarah2/Shutterstock.com (Colorado potato beetle), exOrzist/Shutterstock.com (wasp petiole). 7: Eldred Lim/Shutterstock.com (scorpion), CreativeNature.nl/Shutterstock.com (spider), Eric Isselée/Shutterstock.com (millipede). 8: Elliotte Rusty Harold/Shutterstock.com (European honey bee), Studiotouch/Shutterstock.com (fruit fly). 9: Roger Meerts/Shutterstock.com (lacewing), optimarc/Shutterstock.com (water strider). 10: Yaro/Shutterstock.com (grasshopper), Michael C. Gray/Shutterstock.com (armor), Yory Frenklakh/Shutterstock.com (desert beetle). 11: Don Valentine/Dreamstime.com (cicada), Dirk Sigmund/Dreamstime.com (dragonfly), Four Oaks/Shutterstock.com (dung beetle). 12: Mau Horng/Shutterstock.com (eggs), Jens Stolt/Shutterstock.com (caterpillar). 12–13: Eric Isselée/Shutterstock.com (peacock butterfly). 13: kurt_G/Shutterstock.com (grasshopper nymph), Bruce MacQueen/Shutterstock.com (dragonfly nymph), Minden Pictures/SuperStock (flatid leaf bug nymphs, flatid leaf bug adults). 14: luckypic/Shutterstock.com (cockroach), AP Photo/Mori Chen (locust swarm), AP Photo/Karl-Heinz Kreifelts (goliath beetle). 15: Arto Hakola/Shutterstock.com (froghopper), ©iStockphoto.com/Bruno Combe (termite mound), ©iStockphoto.com/pkgraphics (froghopper larvae), wonderisland/Shutterstock.com (termite queen). 16: kurt_G/Shutterstock.com (giraffe-necked weevil), Nicola Dal Zotto/Shutterstock.com (butterfly scales), ©photooasis/Dreamstime.com (glasswing butterfly). 17: ©Minden Pictures/SuperStock (golden scarab beetle), ©Halil I Inci/Dreamstime.com (hummingbird hawk-moth), kurt_G/Shutterstock.com (trap-jaw ant). 18: argonaut/Shutterstock.com (stag beetle head), Jackiso/Shutterstock.com (beetles fighting). 19: ©Alexei Grishin/Dreamstime.com (grasshopper), ©Minden Pictures/SuperStock (assassin bug), kurt_G/Shutterstock.com (butterfly). 20: ©iStockphoto.com/Erik Svec (beetle head and antenna), Jaykan/Shutterstock.com (jewel beetle), Ultrashock/Shutterstock.com (beetle wings). 21: Alexey Stiop/Shutterstock.com (firefly), johannviloria/Shutterstock.com (bombardier beetle), Mircea BEZERGHEANU/Shutterstock.com (ladybug), ©Minden Pictures/SuperStock (titan beetle), wagtail/Shutterstock.com (Japanese tiger beetle). 22–23: Frank Greenaway/Dorling Kindersley/Getty Images. 22: KULISH VIKTORIIA/Shutterstock.com. 23: James Laurie/Shutterstock.com (monarch butterfly), NCG/Shutterstock.com (monarch migration). 24: Marco Uliana/Shutterstock.com (orange moth), Sari ONeal/Shutterstock.com (butterfly), Ian Maton/Shutterstock.com (multicolored moth). 25: ©age fotostock/SuperStock (sunset moths), ©Eduardo Grund/age fotostock/SuperStock (atlas moth). 26: Mikhail Melnikov/Shutterstock.com (dragonfly eye from the side), biker11/Shutterstock.com (dragonfly eye from the front). 27: Protasov A&N/Shutterstock.com (mango tree borer, close-up of

mango tree borer eye), ©NHPA/SuperStock (honey bee eye), D. Kucharski & K. Kucharska/Shutterstock.com (bee ocelli), Pinosub/Shutterstock.com (mantis ocelli). 28: Lucertolone/Shutterstock.com. 29: Kippy Spilker/Shutterstock.com (bee corbicula), irin-k/Shutterstock.com (wasp), mdlart/Shutterstock.com (bee covered in pollen). 30: ©Premaphotos/Alamy (stink bugs), ©age fotostock/SuperStock (katydid), ©Cusp/SuperStock (thorn bugs). 31: ©Ruby B. Llamas/Dreamstime.com (polka dot wasp moth), Nature Images/Photo Researchers/Getty Images (mydas fly), AP Photo/*The Bakersfield Californian,* Casey Christie (tarantula and wasp), S.J. Krasemann/Peter Arnold/Getty Images (hawk-moth caterpillar). 32: Pan Xunbin/Shutterstock.com (stick insect on branch), Redchanka/Shutterstock.com (Javanese leaf insect), David W. Leindecker/Shutterstock.com (stick insect in hands). 33: alslutsky/Shutterstock.com (Malaysian jungle leaf insect), Andrew Burgess/Shutterstock.com (giant prickly stick). 34: Cathy Keifer/Shutterstock.com (mantis eating, Texas unicorn mantis), Eric Isselee/Shutterstock.com (devil's flower mantis, ghost mantis). 35: WIANGYA/Shutterstock.com (orchid mantis), ©Naturesdisplay/Dreamstime.com (startle display). 36: Roger Meerts/Shutterstock.com (puss moth caterpillar), chinahbzyg/Shutterstock.com (stink bug on left), sunsetman/Shutterstock.com (stink bug on right), Peter Waters/Shutterstock.com (black bulldog ant). 37: ©NHPA/SuperStock (spiny devil katydid), Sean van Tonder/Shutterstock.com (African grasshopper), Jacob Hamblin/Shutterstock.com (monarch caterpillar). 38: SweetCrisis/Shutterstock.com (ant bridge), ©Minden Pictures/SuperStock (leafcutter ants). 39: Gilbert M. Grosvenor/National Geographic Stock (ant bite), Carlo Bavagnoli/Time & Life Picgtures/Getty Images (driver and grasshopper), Anton Gvozdikov/Shutterstock.com (formica ants), Potapov Alexander/Shutterstock.com (ant), irin-k/Shutterstock.com (wasp). 40: Keith Naylor/Shutterstock.com. 41: Ron Rowan Photography/Shutterstock.com (Japanese beetles), Amy Walters/Shutterstock.com (termite damaged wood), D. Kucharski & K. Kucharska/Shutterstock.com (wheat weevil), Henrik Larsson/Shutterstock.com (mosquito), sydeen/Shutterstock.com (termites eating wood). 42: Soyka/Shutterstock.com (hissing cockroach), Smit/Shutterstock.com (group of cockroaches). 43: ©Animals Animals/SuperStock (cockroaches on sandwich), kzww/Shutterstock.com (cockroach underside). 44: ©Minden Pictures/SuperStock (harvester ant), ©Stock Connection/SuperStock (harvester ant nest), aceshot1/Shutterstock.com (chrysalis). 45: Otto Hahn/Picture Press/Getty Images (hornet), argonaut/Shutterstock.com (Arctic beetles), Photo by Jon Sullivan (alpine weta). 46: AP Photo/Sakchai Lalit (serving insects), ©Tips Images/SuperStock (Thailand market), ©NHPA/SuperStock (Zambian market). 47: ©Tips Images/SuperStock (mopane worms), Chad Zuber/Shutterstock.com (chapulines), p.studio66/Shutterstock.com (fried crickets), Yuttasak Jannarong/Shutterstock.com (silkworm larvae). 48: ©Imagemore/SuperStock (stag beetle antennae, stag beetle), ©Andre Skonieczny/imag/imagebroker.net/SuperStock (flower chafer). Back cover: Redchanka/Shutterstock.com (Japanese leaf insect), kurt_G/Shutterstock.com (giraffe-necked weevil), Roger Meerts/Shutterstock.com (puss moth caterpillar), Neale Cousland/Shutterstock.com (butterfly).

Printed in China, April 2013

ISBN 978-1-935703-58-7

10 9 8 7 6 5 4 3 2 1

Downtown Bookworks Inc.
285 West Broadway
New York, NY 10013

www.dtbwpub.com

CONTENTS

INSECTS EVERYWHERE!

Insects are amazing. They can be found on all seven continents and make up more than two-thirds of all known living organisms. There are more types, or species, of insects than any other animal on Earth. There are more than 150,000 different species of flies alone! And scientists are discovering new insects all the time.

Grasshoppers can jump 80 times their body length. This would be like a human jumping over 1.5 football fields.

Rainbow grasshopper

Lantern fly

The scientific study of insects is called entomology. A scientist who specializes in insects is an entomologist.

Tetrio sphinx caterpillar

Entomologists have identified about one million different species of insects. Because some insects live in very hard-to-reach places, are often very small, and are really good at hiding, scientists believe there are hundreds of thousands, maybe even millions, that we haven't even seen yet!

Humans have about 700 muscles. Grasshoppers have 900, and caterpillars may have as many as 4,000!

Stink bug

Cockchafer (Maybug, June beetle)

5

WHAT MAKES AN INSECT
AN INSECT

All insects have a **head, thorax,** and **abdomen.** These three body parts come in many different shapes and sizes, but if you look closely, you'll find them every time.

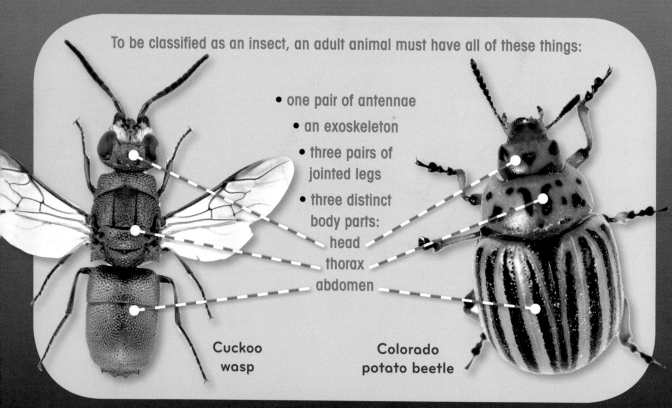

To be classified as an insect, an adult animal must have all of these things:

- one pair of antennae
- an exoskeleton
- three pairs of jointed legs
- three distinct body parts:
  head
  thorax
  abdomen

Cuckoo wasp

Colorado potato beetle

Many wasps have a tiny petiole, or waist, separating their thorax from their abdomen.

Nearly all insects have a pair of compound eyes (see page 26). But some insects that live deep in caves and never see sunlight are blind.

People often mistake spiders, millipedes, centipedes, and scorpions for insects, but scientists have placed these animals in different categories. Spiders, for instance, have eight legs, no antennae, and only one or two body parts. Scorpions also have eight legs. They are related to spiders. Centipedes and millipedes have a lot more than six legs.

Scorpion

Spider

Millipede

Insects have blood, but it's different from ours. Red blood cells give our blood its color and carry oxygen to wherever it is needed in the body. Insects get oxygen from a system of tubes that connect to the outside of their bodies. Instead of carrying oxygen, insect blood carries only nutrients and water. Even though most insects have green or yellowish blood, they do bleed when they are injured, just like us.

NAMING INSECTS

People often call the same insect by different names. To make sure they are talking about the same critter, entomologists use an official two-part name for each insect. The first part of the name is the genus (*jee*-nus). A genus is a group of related animals or organisms. The second name is the species (*spee*-sheez). The species tells you exactly which insect you have.

These names are usually in Latin and often hard to pronounce, like *Apis mellifera* for the European honey bee, or *Drosophila melanogaster* for the fruit fly. Some scientists have fun when they name insects. George Kirkaldy named one insect *Ochisme* (which sounds like "oh kiss me") and another one *Polychisme* ("Polly kiss me"). Other scientists have named a fly *Pieza kake* ("piece of cake") and a wasp *Heerz tooya* ("here's to ya").

Apis mellifera is the scientific name for the European honey bee.

Drosophila melanogaster is the scientific name for the fruit fly.

8

Many insects have a common name or nickname. Honey bee, walking stick, grasshopper, fire ant, lacewing, and stink bug are examples of common names. How many common insect names do you know?

Gerris remigis (water strider or pond skater)

Chrysoperla rufilabris (green lacewing)

Most people use the words *bug* and *insect* to mean the same thing. But the word *bug* actually only refers to one particular type of insect. True bugs have a mouth shaped like a straw, called a stylet. They use their stylet to suck the juices from plants or to slurp up the insides of other animals. Stink bugs, assassin bugs, and water striders are types of true bugs.

LOOK MA, NO BONES!

Insects have no bones. Instead, their soft bodies and organs are protected by an outer shell called an exoskeleton (*exo* means "outside"). Exoskeletons provide insects with excellent protection and strength. An exoskeleton is made up of stiff plates with flexible sections that act as joints so the insect can move. Humans have endoskeletons (*endo* means "inside")—our bones are inside our bodies.

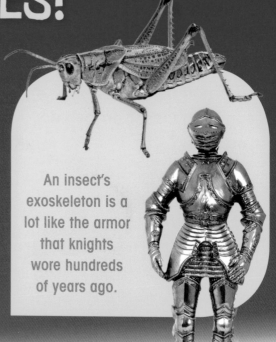

An insect's exoskeleton is a lot like the armor that knights wore hundreds of years ago.

In the animal world, exoskeletons are much more common than endoskeletons—millions of species have exoskeletons, while only a few thousand have endoskeletons.

Insect exoskeletons and human fingernails are made of similar substances. An exoskeleton is hard and waterproof. Most exoskeletons can even protect an insect from strong chemicals and bleach. These hard outer shells also offer insects protection from germs, from being eaten by some predators, and from being hurt when they fall.

During periods of dry weather, exoskeletons keep body moisture from escaping. In wet weather, they help to keep water out.

Exoskeletons don't grow, so an insect must shed its armor to get bigger. When an insect gets large enough, its exoskeleton splits open, and a larger version of the insect emerges, leaving the old exoskeleton behind. The outer layer of the insect's new body will harden into a new exoskeleton, but before their body hardens, they are soft and vulnerable to being attacked by predators.

A cicada emerging from its exoskeleton.

Some dragonflies molt more than 20 times before reaching their final, adult stage.

A dung beetle is so strong, it can pull something 1,141 times heavier than itself. That would be the same as a person dragging around five school buses packed with kids!

The dung beetle's skeleton helps to prevent it from being injured.

GROWING AND CHANGING

Most baby animals look like their parents, only smaller. But some baby insects look completely different from their parents. This is because most insects go through either a complete life cycle or an incomplete life cycle, during which their appearance changes a lot.

Butterfly eggs

During its larval stage, a butterfly is known as a caterpillar.

Caterpillars need to eat a lot so they have enough energy for the next stage of their life cycle. Caterpillars eat leaves, but adult butterflies drink nectar from flowers.

A complete life cycle has four stages: egg, larva, pupa, and adult. Butterflies, mosquitoes, ants, fleas, bees, wasps, and house flies have complete life cycles.

A butterfly begins life as a very small egg. When the egg hatches, it is a very hungry larva. To become a pupa, a caterpillar must make a case for itself, called a chrysalis. Inside the chrysalis, the butterfly goes through a complete transformation, or metamorphosis. After a few days or sometimes after an entire winter, a fully formed adult butterfly emerges, spreads its wings, and flies away.

A peacock butterfly climbs out of its chrysalis.

Grasshopper nymph

Some insects have an incomplete life cycle, which only has three stages: **egg, nymph,** and **adult.** Nymphs often look like miniature adults, but they are not yet able to reproduce. These insects eat the same food as nymphs and adults. Grasshoppers, earwigs, cockroaches, and dragonflies have incomplete life cycles. Nymphs do not have wings, but wing buds develop during this stage. Wings continue to grow larger each time the nymph molts, until they are fully developed.

Dragonfly nymph

Nymph flatid leaf bugs

During their nymph stage, flatid leaf bugs form long strands of a waxlike substance that covers their body, making them appear as if they have white feathers. As adults, they have large, smooth wings.

Adult flatid leaf bugs

AND THE WINNER IS...

The fastest **flying insect** is the dragonfly. The southern giant darner dragonfly can fly as fast as 35 miles per hour.

The fastest insect on the ground is the cockroach. In one study, an American cockroach was clocked at 50 body lengths per second. If a human did that, he or she would be running 210 miles per hour!

The heaviest insect is the goliath beetle, found in Africa's tropical forests. It can weigh as much as 3.5 ounces.

A swarm is a large group of insects that travel together in search of food or a new home. In 1889, the **largest documented swarm of locusts** covered an area of 2,000 square miles. It was estimated to contain 250 billion locusts.

A swarm of locusts in Israel in 2004

Mound-building termites create the **tallest homes**. Mounds in Africa have reached 42 feet in height. That's about as tall as a four-story building!

A high-speed camera has revealed that the **most powerful jumper in the insect world** is the froghopper. This little critter can jump more than two feet and accelerate at an incredible 13,000 feet per second. If humans could do this, we would be able to jump over skyscrapers that are 70 stories tall!

This termite mound is **much taller than a person.**

Froghoppers are also known as spittlebugs, because their larvae hide from predators under a foamy substance that looks like spit.

Queen termites grow to be too big to walk or fly.

Termite queens have been known to live for 50 years, and some scientists believe they may live as long as 100 years. They are the **longest-living insects.**

15

LOOK AT THAT!

Insects come in many different shapes, sizes, and colors. Check out these fascinating insects and their special features.

The giraffe-necked weevil, from Madagascar, is a head above the rest. The male uses his long neck to roll up leaves for his mate. His mate will lay a single egg inside the tube.

Butterfly scales up close

Most butterflies have tiny colored scales on their wings. These scales make up beautiful and intricate designs. Glasswing butterflies do not have these scales, so their wings are see-through.

The golden scarab beetle is a dung beetle that inspired a myth in ancient Egypt. According to the story, a huge golden scarab rolled the sun across the sky every day, much like another dung beetle might roll a ball of dung across the ground.

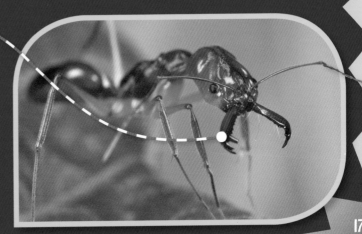

This hummingbird hawk-moth, or hummingmoth, looks and acts a lot like a hummingbird. Its proboscis, which is kind of like a tube-shaped tongue (see page 19), can measure up to 13 inches in length!

The trap-jaw ant has the fastest bite on the planet. It can snap its mandibles (see page 18) shut at 145 miles per hour. That's 2,300 times faster than you can blink your eye! It can also use its powerful jaws to toss itself into the air and away from a predator.

MUNCH, SLURP, GRAB

MANDIBLES

MAXILLAE

Stag beetle

Male stag beetles use their enormous mandibles to fight with each other.

An insect's mouth is made up of a bunch of "mouthparts." These parts work together to help chew, drink, taste, fight, and even build homes.

Insects that chew their food have two jaws called mandibles. Mandibles have sharp, bumpy edges and are designed for slicing and biting. Unlike human jaws, mandibles move side to side. Behind the mandibles are two parts called maxillae that help to hold food and move it into the insect's mouth. Attached to the maxillae are the palps. These are used for tasting.

Mouthparts are shaped differently on different insects. Some insects, like the grasshopper, have "lips" called the **labrum** and **labium** that cover their mouthparts. Bees, moths, butterflies, and many flies have maxillae that form into a long, hollow tube called a **proboscis.** They use the proboscis like a straw to drink nectar from flowers.

Some insects have a **stylet,** which they use to pierce their food and suck out the fluids. Assassin bugs, aphids, and mosquitoes have stylets.

A grasshopper's labrum is like an upper lip, and its labium is like a bottom lip. It also has a pair of palps.

A butterfly's proboscis is so long, it must be coiled up when the insect is not eating.

An assassin bug uses its stylet to suck out the insides of a beetle.

BEETLES

There are more than 400,000 known species of beetles in the world. No other type of insect has that much variety.

The beautiful outer wings of the jewel beetle are treasured by many cultures and used to make jewelry and adorn clothing.

Adult beetles have two sets of wings. The first set is hard and acts as a protective covering. Underneath these hard wings is a pair of wings that are transparent, or see-through. Many beetles can fly with their second wings.

Most beetles don't see very well, so they communicate through scent, sound, and vibration. They can make noise by scraping their mouthparts, rubbing their legs against their bodies, or tapping on dead wood. Some beetles are predators, which means that they hunt, and others are scavengers, which means they eat what they find. Most beetles live about a year, but some of the larger ones can live longer.

Fireflies belong to the beetle family. They communicate with each other by glowing.

Crushed beetle shells have been used in makeup since Cleopatra was alive more than 2,000 years ago!

When threatened, the bombardier beetle squirts a hot toxic gas out of an opening in its abdomen.

Japanese tiger beetle

Ladybug

The titan beetle, a type of longhorn beetle from South America, can grow to be 6.6 inches long. That's probably bigger than your foot!

21

BIG, BEAUTIFUL WINGS

March 14 is Learn About Butterflies Day!

Butterflies have been fluttering around and drinking the nectar from flowers since the days of dinosaurs.

The Queen Alexandra's birdwing is the largest known butterfly. The females, which are larger than the males, can grow to be 12 inches across. Discovered in 1906, they were named after Alexandra, the wife of Britain's King Edward VII. The word *birdwing* refers to their birdlike size.

These rare butterflies are only found in the rain forests of Papua New Guinea and are in danger of going extinct.

LIFE SIZE!

A female Queen Alexandra's birdwing

Many butterflies have patterns on their wings that look like eyes. This can scare off predators.

Monarch butterfly

A butterfly cannot fly if its body temperature is less than 86°F.

Flying up to a record 17 miles per hour, the mighty monarch butterfly is the fastest butterfly. Similar to many birds, monarchs travel in large groups, migrating in order to lay their eggs far away from where they are born. They can travel up to 2,000 miles in a lifetime. That's the distance from New York City to Mexico! They can even fly for 44 hours without stopping.

BUTTERFLIES VS. MOTHS

Although butterflies and moths are very similar, there are many differences between them.

Most butterflies are active during the day, and most moths are active at night. When resting, butterflies usually hold their wings up, whereas moths open up their wings to lie nearly flat. Butterfly wings are usually more colorful than moth wings. Most butterfly bodies are slender and hairless. In contrast, moths are fat and furry. Moths have existed for about 100 million years longer than butterflies.

Most moth antennae look like feathers or threads, while butterfly antennae are thin with a thicker knob on the end. Moths use these amazing antennae to detect their partners from miles away.

Butterfly

Moth

Some people say the sunset moth, found in Madagascar, is the most beautiful insect in the world.

Just like bees and flies, butterflies and moths taste with their feet.

The atlas moth is one of the largest moths. Their cocoons are so big that some people in Taiwan use them as coin purses!

HOW INSECTS SEE THE WORLD

A dragonfly's eyes cover most of its head.

Insects cannot see very far away or make out the details of the things around them. But their eyes can detect the slightest changes in light and movement. This ability helps insects avoid being swatted, squished, or eaten by predators.

Insect eyes are so different from our own that it's hard for scientists to imagine how the world appears to an insect. Almost all adult insects have two compound eyes that are made up of many small lenses or "mini eyes" that see separate images. Each tiny lens has six sides. The lenses fit together perfectly, like a honeycomb.

Humans have only one lens in each eye. Dragonflies have as many as 30,000!

Insect eyes don't move. Insects see more colors than humans see.

An extreme close-up of the compound eye of a mango tree borer

Insects also have simple eyes, called ocelli, which detect light and dark. Many adult insects have three ocelli between their compound eyes. Most immature insects, like caterpillars, do not have compound eyes. Instead, they have many ocelli. Some insects even have special light-sensing cells on the sides of their body to help them understand what is happening around them. Cockroaches have these special cells all along their sides.

Honey bees have hairs on their eyes that help them gauge the speed and direction of the wind as they fly.

Can you see the trio of dots on the bee and the mantis? Those are the animals' ocelli.

HONEY BEES

Many bees live alone, but honey bees are considered social insects, because they live and work in large groups. A group of honey bees is called a **colony.** Honey bee colonies make intricate hives.

Each cell, or opening, in the honeycomb is perfectly shaped with six sides. These cells are used to store honey, eggs, and larvae.

Honey bees are expert engineers. Worker bees secrete beeswax from glands in their abdomen. Then they shape the wax into honeycombs.

Most bee species have stingers, but only the females can sting. And most species of bees cannot pierce human skin.

When a honey bee finds a good supply of pollen and nectar, it returns to the hive and does a special dance. The way the bee wiggles during the dance tells other bees where to find the source of food.

There is one fertile, egg-laying female bee in each honey bee colony, and she is called the **queen.** She can lay up to 2,000 eggs a day for two to three years! **Drones** are male bees that mate with the queen. Generally, there are thousands of **worker bees** that collect pollen and nectar and tend to the hive. When bees visit a flower to drink nectar, their furry little bodies become covered in dusty pollen. When they visit a new flower, some pollen falls off. This process, called **pollination,** enables the flower to produce seeds. Insects—and honey bees in particular—are the greatest plant pollinators in the world. Without them, most plant and animal life would be in danger of extinction.

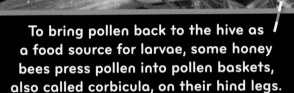

To bring pollen back to the hive as a food source for larvae, some honey bees press pollen into pollen baskets, also called corbicula, on their hind legs.

Wasps are not bees. Almost all wasps are meat eaters, and bees feed on flowers. In general, wasps are not as hairy as bees.

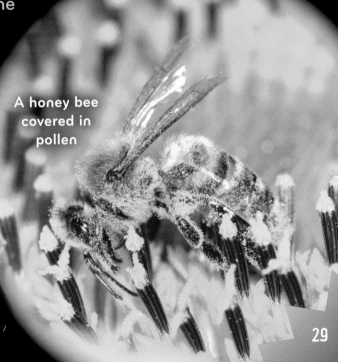

A honey bee covered in pollen

29

MIMICRY AND CAMOUFLAGE

Many insects blend into their environment as a form of protection. Some alter their appearance to look like leaves or branches. Others scare off predators with markings and behaviors that mimic bigger and more dangerous animals.

These stink bugs are masters of camouflage. They blend into their surroundings. Can you find all of them?

Not only does this katydid look like a leaf, but it looks like a leaf that has been munched on by another insect.

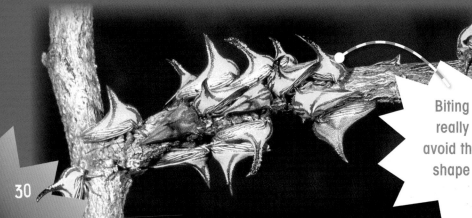

Biting into a thorny plant can really hurt, so many animals avoid them. That's why the spiky shape of a thorn bug helps to keep it safe.

Polka dot wasp moth

Mydas fly

The polka dot wasp moth (also called the oleander moth) and the mydas fly are both harmless insects that look like stinging wasps. They even mimic the jerky movements of wasps, but they have no actual stingers. Many species of flies, moths, and longhorn beetles mimic bees and wasps.

The mydas fly looks a lot like the tarantula hawk wasp, which has venom so powerful, it can stun a tarantula with a single sting.

Tarantula hawk wasp

Hawk moth caterpillars have markings that look like the eyes of a much larger animal. As if that isn't enough to freak out a potential predator, some of these caterpillars can also alter their body shape so it resembles the head of a snake.

TWIGS AND LEAVES . . . WITH LEGS

When stick insects hang from a branch, they move very slowly. Sometimes, they rock back and forth so they look like branches swaying in the breeze. This is also why they are often called "walking sticks." They can range in size from ½ inch to more than 21 inches long when their legs are extended!

Stick insects are found mostly in tropical and subtropical climates. The males and females often look different. The females are usually larger, while the males are thinner.

Javanese leaf insect

It is easier to spot stick insects when they are away from leaves and branches.

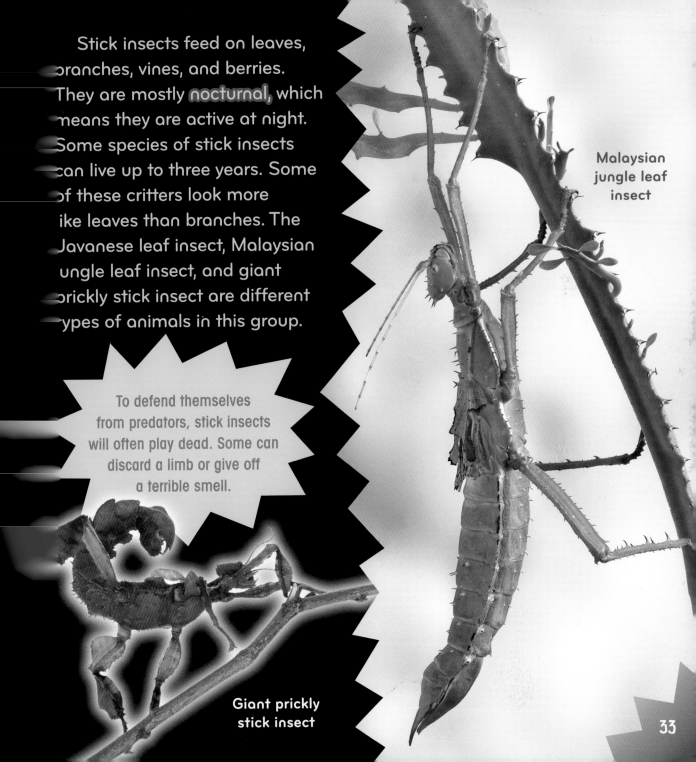

Stick insects feed on leaves, branches, vines, and berries. They are mostly nocturnal, which means they are active at night. Some species of stick insects can live up to three years. Some of these critters look more like leaves than branches. The Javanese leaf insect, Malaysian jungle leaf insect, and giant prickly stick insect are different types of animals in this group.

To defend themselves from predators, stick insects will often play dead. Some can discard a limb or give off a terrible smell.

Malaysian jungle leaf insect

Giant prickly stick insect

PRAYING MANTISES

Praying mantises are master hunters. Their coloring and wing shape help them camouflage themselves as flowers, grass, wood, and dead leaves while they wait for unsuspecting prey. These carnivores eat other insects, but the larger species are mighty enough to hunt down small rodents, lizards, tree frogs, hummingbirds, and even snakes!

Devil's flower mantis

Texas unicorn mantis

Ghost mantis

Deep in the jungles of Malaysia and Indonesia, the orchid mantis thrives among the delicate flowers of the tropical rain forest. Instead of hunting, it waits for insects to come looking for flower nectar and then attacks them. A mantis's colors and body parts can look like different parts of nearby flowers.

Orchid mantis

Female mantises are larger than the males. Sometimes, the females eat the males after mating.

Mantises can turn their heads 180 degrees, allowing them to look directly behind themselves. When a mantis is in danger, it takes this pose, called a startle display. Some also fill their abdomen with air so they can hiss like a snake. This is often enough to send most predators running in the opposite direction.

Startle display

STAYING ALIVE

Insects have survived for millions of years—through ice ages, volcanic eruptions, droughts, and attacks from lots of hungry predators. Over time, they've developed some pretty nifty ways of staying alive.

The puss moth caterpillar is the most dangerous caterpillar in Britain. When threatened, it extends two of its back legs. The legs change color as a warning. Then the caterpillar sprays acid in the face of its attacker.

Almost every critter on the planet likes to eat insects, so insects need effective ways to avoid being eaten. Some insects trick predators into thinking they are larger by spreading their wings or puffing up body parts. Some insects bite, sting, or poison potential predators. Some force air out of tiny holes to make hissing noises, while other species work together like an army to fight off an attacker.

There is a group of true bugs (see page 9) known as stink bugs, that produce a liquid that gives off a terrible smell. No one wants a stinky meal.

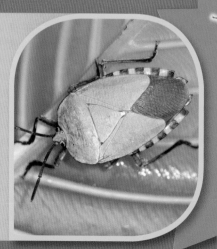

The black bulldog ant, from Australia, is one of the most poisonous insects on the planet. They bite and sting at the same time and have been known to cause death in humans.

Spiny devil katydids have ears on their knees!

The spiny devil katydid lives in Central and South American rain forests. It is covered in sharp spines, making it a painful snack for any predator.

This African grasshopper's coloring warns other animals that it will taste bad.

Lots of poisonous insects display warning colors, which are contrasting colors that tell other animals to stay away. Many African grasshoppers and some butterflies, including the monarch and Queen Alexandra's birdwing (see pages 22–23), eat poisonous plants. They store the plant poisons in their bodies, and predators avoid eating them.

A monarch caterpillar munches on the poisonous milkweed plant. It will keep the poison in its body through adulthood.

37

ANTS WORK TOGETHER

Ants team up to create a bridge from one leaf to the next.

Leafcutter ants cut off pieces of leaf to carry back to their colony.

Ants live on every continent but Antarctica. If it were possible to put all of the world's ants on a scale and weigh them, they'd be heavier than all of the people on Earth. That's a lot of ants!

Within an ant colony, or group, each ant has a specific job to do.

Some ants take care of the eggs. Some build the nest. Some hunt or forage for food, and some defend the nest. Worker ants work as a group, sweeping the forest floor for food to bring back to the nest. They spread out in a fan shape to overpower other insects, scorpions, spiders, and animals much larger than themselves.

Most ants are nearly blind and communicate with each other using movement, scent, and their antennae. Their legs are covered in special hairs that make them very sensitive to touch.

A scientist shows how he uses an ant's bite to help close up a cut or wound.

The jaws of some soldier ants are so strong that they have been used by doctors to close up wounds. While holding two sides of a wound together, a doctor allows the ant to bite into the skin. Then, the doctor rips off the ant's body. The ant's head remains, and its closed jaws can hold a wound closed for a few days.

A driver ant attacks a grasshopper.

Formica ants

Ants are closely related to bees and wasps.

39

HELPFUL INSECTS AND PESTS

Aphid

Ladybug

Many insects are helpful to us and our environment. In fact, we'd be in real trouble without them. For example, bees and butterflies help pollinate plants, which is how plants reproduce. Blow flies, carrion beetles, and other insects called **decomposers** eat dead plants and animals. They break these things into tiny pieces that can return to the soil and be used to nourish new plants and animals.

Farmers call aphids pests because they kill plants by sucking the juice out of them. Ladybugs are considered helpful, because they love to eat aphids. A single ladybug can eat 5,000 aphids in its lifetime!

When insects do things that humans don't like, we call them pests. Aphids, weevils, stink bugs, and locusts eat our crops. Locusts are not common in the United States anymore, but in Africa, Europe, and Asia, a large swarm might eat 80,000 tons of grain and other vegetation in a day. Some wood-eating termites eat the wood in our homes.

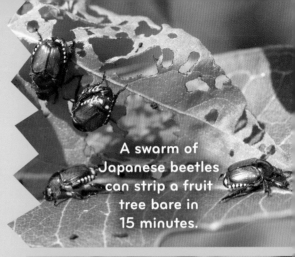

A swarm of Japanese beetles can strip a fruit tree bare in 15 minutes.

Mosquito

Not only are mosquito bites unpleasant, but they can be dangerous. Mosquitoes can carry diseases, including malaria. Mostly found in Africa, malaria is one of the most deadly illnesses known to humans. Some flies can also pass diseases to humans when they bite.

Wheat weevils cause lots of damage to wheat fields.

Termite-damaged wood

Termites eating wood

41

COCKROACHES

Although they look like beetles, cockroaches are in a group all their own.

These amazing insects are practically indestructible. They've been around since before the dinosaurs and can be found in just about every habitat on Earth. They are able to hide in teeny-tiny spaces and can run faster than any other insect. They can also handle six times the amount of radiation that would kill a human. This means that cockroaches can even survive the aftermath of a nuclear bomb!

Hissing cockroaches, from Madagascar, make noise by pushing air out of their spiracles, or breathing holes. They live in the forest.

About 99% of cockroaches live on the forest floor and are not pests.

Cockroaches are scavengers, which means they eat what they find—and they'll eat almost anything, including paint, paper, and soap. They can even digest wood. Catching a cockroach isn't easy. They are incredibly sensitive to vibrations and can feel you coming as soon as you start shifting your weight. They like to live in the dark, and they have special, light-sensitive cells on the sides of their bodies. If the lights are suddenly turned on, they quickly scurry out of sight.

A female German cockroach can lay thousands of eggs during her five months of life.

If a cockroach loses its head, it can still survive for a week (possibly even a month) before dying of dehydration. That's because only part of its brain is in its head. The rest is in the lower part of its body.

SURVIVING THE WINTER

Insects are cold-blooded, which means that instead of making their own body heat, they must absorb heat from the environment in order to survive. So, how do they live through the winter? Many insects either stay underground or travel to warmer climates during the cold winter months. Others have developed incredible ways to survive in freezing temperatures.

Harvester ants make a special storage space deep in their nests and then collect a huge amount of food to last through the winter when there are no leaves or buds outside for them to eat.

Many **moths** and **butterflies** remain in the pupa stage during the winter. Protected by the hard covering of a cocoon or chrysalis, these pupae can rest underground or even tucked under tree bark. The adult moth or butterfly will then emerge in the spring.

Out of a whole colony of hornets, only the fertilized females, known as queens, will live through the winter. When the other members of the nest start to die off, the queen finds a sheltered spot underground or in a tree and waits until spring to lay her eggs. Then she will begin a whole new colony.

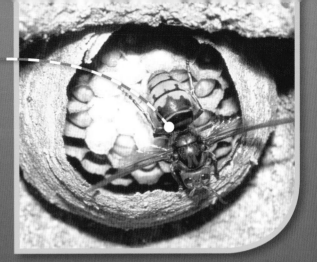

To survive the bitter cold of an Arctic winter, the bodies of Arctic beetles actually produce antifreeze. As temperatures drop, this beetle replaces some of the water in its body with glycerol. This chemical allows the beetle to withstand temperatures of 14°F without turning into a beetle popsicle.

The alpine weta spends the winter frozen solid! Its heart stops beating and brain stops functioning until it thaws out in the spring and begins moving again.

INSECTS YOU CAN EAT

You may think that eating an insect is something you would only do for big bucks on a reality TV show. In many other parts of the world, people regularly eat insects and even consider them to be special treats!

Insects—they're what's for dinner.

Not all insects are safe to eat, but some are quite good for you. They are usually low in fat and packed with protein and nutrients. Edible insects are also easier and cheaper to farm than other meat. If you'd like to try some, you might like barbecue-flavored mealworms, chocolate-covered silkworm larvae, or spicy giant bug paste. Foods made from insects can be found online or in special shops.

Never eat an insect you find on your own. Edible insects are specially raised and prepared to be food.

Insects for sale at a street market in Thailand

Caterpillars are sold alongside mushrooms and loquat fruits in Zambia.

Street vendors in parts of Asia sell cricket skewers and dragonfly soup. In Mexico, people eat ant eggs, locusts, and caterpillars. Chapulines is a popular Mexican dish of grasshoppers roasted in chili and lime. In southern Africa, a dinner of mopane worms is so special that it's more expensive than steak.

Mopane worms

The practice of eating insects is called entomophagy.

Chapulines are both delicious and packed with protein and calcium.

Many people say fried crickets taste like popcorn, potato chips, or pine nuts.

In Asia, silkworm larvae are eaten canned, boiled, steamed, roasted, stir-fried, and deep-fried.

Cooked stink bugs are sweet. Some say they taste sort of like apples.

SEE A LITTLE CRITTER UP CLOSE!

Insect-O-Mania comes with a special treasure just for you: a beetle perfectly preserved in resin. You will either find a stag beetle or a flower chafer.

There are about 1,200 species of stag beetles living around the world, mostly in rain forests. In most of these species, the males and females look different. The males are larger and have bigger mandibles that they use for fighting other males. Stag beetles lay their eggs in rotting wood.

Despite its bulky body, flower chafers are able to fly very fast.

Stag beetles have peculiar antennae. The first section of the antennae is the thinnest. And there is a wide, comb-like club at the end.

If you find a flower chafer in your book, hold it up to a light and see how its metallic exoskeleton glitters. There are nearly 4,000 different types of flower chafers around the world. Like many other beetles, flower chafers can fly. The hard outer wings that you see in your specimen are called the elytra. Tucked underneath the elytra are the see-through wings that the flower chafer uses for flying.